Fast & Easy Instant Pot Seafood & Fish Cookbook
50 Craving-Satisfied Recipes for Seafood Lovers
Johanna Davis

Text Copyright © Johanna Davis

All rights reserved. No part of this guide may be reproduced in any form without permission in writing from the publisher except in the case of brief quotations embodied in critical articles or reviews.

Legal & Disclaimer

The information contained in this book and its contents is not designed to replace or take the place of any form of medical or professional advice; and is not meant to replace the need for independent medical, financial, legal or other professional advice or services, as may be required. The content and information in this book has been provided for educational and entertainment purposes only.

The content and information contained in this book has been compiled from sources deemed reliable, and it is accurate to the best of the Author's knowledge, information and belief. However, the Author cannot guarantee its accuracy and validity and cannot be held liable for any errors and/or omissions. Further, changes are periodically made to this book as and when needed. Where appropriate and/or necessary, you must consult a professional (including but not limited to your doctor, attorney, financial advisor or such other professional advisor) before using any of the suggested remedies, techniques, or information in this book.

Upon using the contents and information contained in this book, you agree to hold harmless the Author from and against any damages, costs, and expenses, including any legal fees potentially resulting from the application of any of the information provided by this book. This disclaimer applies to any loss, damages or injury caused by the use and application, whether directly or indirectly, of any advice or information presented, whether for breach of contract, tort, negligence, personal injury, criminal intent, or under any other cause of action.

You agree to accept all risks of using the information presented inside this book.
You agree that by continuing to read this book, where appropriate and/or necessary, you shall consult a professional (including but not limited to your doctor, attorney, or financial advisor or such other advisor as needed) before using any of the suggested remedies, techniques, or information in this book.

Table of Contents

Chapter 1 Cooking Fish and Seafood

Chapter 2 Fish and Seafood Recipes

    Chapter 2.1   Shrimp Dishes

        Recipe 1: <u>Classic Garlic Shrimp</u>

        Recipe 2: <u>Shrimp and Crab Stew</u>

        Recipe 3: <u>Shrimp Stir-Fry</u>

        Recipe 4: <u>Butter Shrimp with Asparagus</u>

        Recipe 5: <u>Shrimp Zoodles</u>

        Recipe 6: <u>Shrimp with Asparagus</u>

        Recipe 7: <u>Cajun Shrimp with Asparagus</u>

        Recipe 8: <u>Prawn Curry</u>

        Recipe 9: <u>Lemon-Garlic Prawns</u>

        Recipe 10: <u>Shrimp and Tomato Casserole</u>

    Chapter 2.2   Crab & Lobster Dishes

        Recipe 11: <u>Simple Crab Legs</u>

        Recipe 12: <u>Crab Legs with Butter Sauce</u>

        Recipe 13: <u>Crab Bisque</u>

        Recipe 14: <u>Shrimp, and Crab, with Sausage</u>

        Recipe 15: <u>Lemon Butter Lobster Tail</u>

        Recipe 16: <u>Steamed Lobster Tails</u>

        Recipe 17: <u>Lobster Bisque</u>

Chapter 2.3   Salmon Dishes

Recipe 18: Lemon Dill Salmon

Recipe 19: Salmon Burger with Avocado

Recipe 20: Foil Pack Salmon

Recipe 21: Almond Pesto Salmon

Recipe 22: Crispy Blackened Salmon

Recipe 23: Salmon with Broccoli

Recipe 24: Salmon with Vegetables

Recipe 25: Poached Salmon

Recipe 26: Sockeye Salmon

Recipe 27: Italian Salmon

Chapter 2.4   Tuna & Cod Dishes

Recipe 28: Garlic Tuna Patties

Recipe 29: Almond Tuna

Recipe 30: Olive Cod Mystery

Recipe 31: Tomato Cod

Recipe 32: Coconut Milk Cod

Chapter 2.5   Other Fishes Dishes

    Recipe 33: Creamy Haddock

    Recipe 34: Haddock and Cheddar

    Recipe 35: Caramelized Tilapia

    Recipe 36: Mackerel with Tomatoes

    Recipe 37: Fish Taco Bowls

    Recipe 38: Herbed Catfish

    Recipe 39: White Fish Stew

    Recipe 40: Mahi Mahi

    Recipe 41: Dijon Halibut

    Recipe 42: Trout Casserole

Chapter 2.6   Other Seafood Dishes

    Recipe 43: Wonder Wine Clams

    Recipe 44: Steamed Clams

    Recipe 45: Clambake

    Recipe 46: Buttered Scallops

    Recipe 47: Oysters

    Recipe 48: Seafood Gumb

    Recipe 49: Seafood Paella

    Recipe 50: Seafood Stew

Chapter 3 Conclusion

CHAPTER 1: COOKING FISH AND SEAFOOD

General cooking tips:
1. Instant Pot doesn't cook your food instantly! It reduces cooking time about 30%.
2. Depending on the food and volume, prepare to spend a few minutes extra for each recipe.
3. Join various online Instant Pot groups and community for troubleshooting questions and recipe inspiration.

Seafood specific tips:
1. Cooking time for fish and seafood is brief.
2. Stewing or steaming is the best cooking method when cooking seafood in the Instant Pot.
3. For steaming, add at least 1 cup water to the Instant Pot. Place the fish in a bowl and place the bowl on a trivet and steam.
4. Do manual release to prevent overcooking.
5. You can cook frozen seafood in the Instant Pot. Add 2 minutes of extra cooking time for frozen items.

Type of Seafood/ Fish	Fresh Cook Time (Minutes)	Frozen Cook Time (Minutes)
Shrimp/Prawn	1-3	2-4
Crab (whole)	2-3	4-5
Lobster	2-3	3-4
Fish (whole)	4-5	5-7
Fish (steak)	3-4	4-6
Fish (fillet)	2-3	3-4
Mussels	1-2	2-3
Seafood soup/stock	7-8	8-9

CHAPTER 2: FISH AND SEAFOOD RECIPES
Chapter 2.1   Shrimp Dishes

Recipe 1: Classic Garlic Shrimp

| Prep time: 10 minutes | Cook time: 5 minutes | Servings: 4 |

Nutritional Facts Per Serving
- Calories: 244
- Fat: 10g
- Carb: 3.5g
- Protein: 33g

Ingredients
- Coconut oil – 2 Tbsp.
- Chopped parsley – 3 Tbsp.
- Juice of 1 lemon
- Shrimp – 1 ½ pound, peeled and deveined
- Chicken broth – ¾ cup
- Garlic cloves – 3, minced

Method
1. Press Sauté and add oil. Add garlic and stir-fry for 2 minutes or until softened.
2. Add the shrimp and chicken broth.
3. Close the lid and press Manual. Cook for 2 minutes.
4. Do a quick release and open. Add lemon juice and parsley and serve.

Recipe 2: Shrimp and Crab Stew

| Prep time: 10 minutes | Cook time: 15 minutes | Servings: 4 |

Nutritional Facts Per Serving
- Calories: 326
- Fat: 15.4g
- Carb: 3.2g
- Protein: 28.3g

Ingredients
- Coconut oil – 1 Tbsp.
- Onion – ½, diced
- Minced garlic – 2 cloves
- Chopped celery – 2 stalks
- Bay leaf – 1
- Old Bay seasoning – 2 tsp.
- Salt – 1 tsp.
- Shrimp – 1 pound, shelled, deveined, and chopped
- Lump crab meat – 1 pound
- Seafood stock – 4 cups
- Butter – 2 Tbsp.
- Heavy cream – ¼ cup

Method
1. Heat the coconut oil on Sauté in the Instant Pot.
2. Add onions and sauté for 3 minutes.
3. Add garlic and sauté for 30 seconds.
4. Press Cancel.
5. Except for the heavy cream, add all remaining ingredients.
6. Close the lid and press Manual.
7. Cook 10 minutes on High.
8. Do a quick release and stir in heavy cream.
9. Serve.

Recipe 3: Shrimp Stir-Fry

| Prep time: 10 minutes | Cook time: 10 minutes | Servings: 4 |

Nutritional Facts Per Serving
- Calories: 173
- Fat: 7.4g
- Carb: 7g
- Protein: 19.3g

Ingredients
- Coconut oil – 2 Tbsp.
- Medium shrimp – 1 pound, shelled and deveined
- Button mushrooms – ½ cup
- Diced zucchini – ½ cup
- Broccoli florets – 2 cups
- Liquid aminos – ¼ cup
- Minced garlic – 2 cloves
- Red pepper flakes – 1/8 tsp.
- Cooked cauliflower rice – 2 cups

Method
1. Heat the coconut oil on Sauté in the Instant Pot.

2. Add shrimp and stir-fry until fully cooked, about 5 minutes. Remove and set aside.

3. Add red pepper flakes, garlic, liquid aminos, broccoli, zucchini, and mushrooms. Stir-fry for 3 to 5 minutes.

4. Add shrimp back to pot and press cancel.

5. Serve with cauliflower rice.

Recipe 4: Butter Shrimp with Asparagus

| Prep time: 5 minutes | Cook time: 3 minutes | Servings: 2 |

Nutritional Facts Per Serving
- Calories: 381
- Fat: 23.2g
- Carb: 4.3g
- Protein: 32.7g

Ingredients
- Prepared shrimp – 1 pound
- Minced garlic – 1 clove
- Salt – ½ tsp.
- Pepper – ¼ tsp.
- Paprika – ¼ tsp.
- Red pepper flakes – 1/8 tsp.
- Asparagus – ½ pound, cut into bite-sized pieces
- Juice of ½ lemon
- Butter – 4 Tbsp.
- Chopped fresh parsley – 2 tsp.
- Water – 1 cup

Method
1. Sprinkle shrimp with red pepper flakes, paprika, pepper, salt, and garlic.
2. Place in a bowl and add asparagus.
3. Drizzle with lemon juice and mix.
4. Place cubed butter around the dish.
5. Sprinkle with parsley and cover with foil.
6. Add water to the Instant Pot and place steam rack.
7. Place the dish on the steam rack and close the lid.
8. Press Steam and cook 3 minutes.
9. Do a quick release.
10. Remove and serve.

Recipe 5: Shrimp Zoodles

| Prep time: 5 minutes | Cook time: 5 minutes | Servings: 4 |

Nutritional Facts Per Serving
- Calories: 300
- Fat: 20g
- Carb: 3g
- Protein: 30g

Ingredients
- Zoodles – 4 cups
- Ghee – 2 tbsp.
- Veggie stock – 1 cup
- Olive oil – 2 tbsp.
- Minced garlic – 3 tsp.
- Shrimp – 1 pound, peeled and deveined
- Juice of ½ lemon
- Chopped basil – 1 tbsp.
- Paprika – ½ tsp.

Method
1. Melt the ghee along with olive oil in the instant pot on Sauté.
2. Add garlic and cook for 1 minute.
3. Add shrimp and lemon juice.
4. Cook for 1 minute.
5. Add stock, paprika, and zoodles.
6. Cook on High for 3 minutes.
7. Serve topped with basil.
8. Enjoy.

Recipe 6: Shrimp with Asparagus

| Prep time: 5 minutes | Cook time: 2 minutes | Servings: 4 |

Nutritional Facts Per Serving
- Calories: 330
- Total Fats: 7g
- Net Carbs: 7g
- Protein: 45g

Ingredients
- Cajun seasoning – 1 tbsp.
- Shrimp – 1 pound, peeled and deveined
- Asparagus – 1 bunch, trimmed
- Olive oil – 1 tsp.
- Salt and pepper to taste

Method
1. Pour the water into the instant pot.
2. On the instant pot's rack, arrange the asparagus in a single layer.
3. Top with the shrimp.
4. Drizzle with oil and season with salt, pepper, and Cajun.
5. Close the lid and cook for 2 minutes on Steam.
6. Do a quick pressure release.
7. Serve.

Recipe 7: Cajun Shrimp with Asparagus

| Prep time: 5 minutes | Cook time: 2 minutes | Servings: 4 |

Nutritional Facts Per Serving
- Calories: 330
- Fat: 7g
- Carb: 7g
- Protein: 45g

Ingredients
- Cajun seasoning – 1 tbsp.
- Shrimp – 1 pound, peeled and deveined
- Asparagus – 1 bunch, trimmed
- Olive oil – 1 tsp.
- Salt and pepper to taste

Method
1. Pour the water into the IP.
2. Arrange the asparagus in a single layer on the IP's rack.
3. Top with the shrimp.
4. Drizzle with oil and season with Cajun, salt and pepper.
5. Close the lid and cook on Steam for 2 minutes.
6. Do a quick pressure release.
7. Serve.

Recipe 8: Prawn Curry

| Prep time: 5 minutes | Cook time: 10 minutes | Servings: 4 |

Nutritional Facts Per Serving
- Calories: 344
- Fat: 8.5g
- Carb: 7.7g
- Protein: 55g

Ingredients
- Prawns – 2 lbs. peeled and deveined
- Large onion – 1, chopped
- Cloves – 2 garlic, minced
- Coriander leaves – ½ cup, chopped
- Olive oil – 1 tbsp.
- Fish stock – 2 cups
- Fresh ginger – 1 tbsp. grated
- Turmeric powder – ½ tsp.
- Red chili powder – ¼ tsp.
- Cinnamon – ¼ tsp. ground
- Salt – ½ tsp.

Method
1. Grease the stainless steel insert with olive oil.
2. Press the Sauté button and add prawns. Cook 2 to 3 minutes on each side.
3. Add the onions, garlic and all the spices. Stir-fry for 2 more minutes.
4. Add fish stock and coriander. Stir and lock the lid.
5. Adjust the steam release handle and press the Manual button.
6. Set the timer for 5 minutes and cook on High pressure.
7. Do a quick release.
8. Open the pot and transfer the curry to a serving pot.
9. Sprinkle with green onions or fresh parsley and serve.

Recipe 9: Lemon-Garlic Prawns

| Prep time: 5 minutes | Cook time: 5 minutes | Servings: 4 |

Nutritional Facts Per Serving
- Calories: 160
- Fat: 2g
- Carb: 2g
- Protein: 18g

Ingredients
- Minced garlic – 2 tbsp.
- Olive oil – 2 tbsp.
- Lemon zest – 2 tbsp.
- Lemon juice – 2 tbsp.
- Ghee – 1 tbsp.
- Prawns – 1 pound
- Fish stock – 2/3 cup
- Salt and pepper to taste

Method
1. Melt the ghee along with oil in the Instant Pot on Sauté.
2. Add the remaining ingredients and stir to combine.
3. Close the lid and cook on High for 3 minutes.
4. Drain the prawns and serve.

Recipe 10: Shrimp and Tomato Casserole

| Prep time: 5 minutes | Cook time: 16 minutes | Servings: 4 |

Nutritional Facts Per Serving
- Calories: 300
- Fat: 16g
- Carb: 8g
- Protein: 22g

Ingredients
- Shrimp – 1 ½ pounds, peeled and deveined
- Tomatoes – 1 ½ pounds, chopped
- Olive oil – 2 tbsp.
- Veggie broth – ½ cup
- Chopped cilantro – ¼ cup
- Lime juice – 2 tbsp.
- Jalapeno – 1, diced
- Onion – 1, diced
- Shredded cheddar cheese – 1 cup
- Minced garlic – 1 tsp.

Method
1. Press Sauté, and add oil in the IP.
2. Add onion and cook for 3 minutes.
3. Add garlic and sauté for about 1 minute.
4. Stir in tomatoes, cilantro, and broth.
5. Close the lid and cook for High for 9 minutes.
6. Do a natural pressure release.
7. Add shrimp and jalapeno. Cook on High for 2 minutes.
8. Release pressure quickly and stir in cheddar.
9. Drizzle with lemon juice and serve.

Chapter 2.2   Crab & Lobster Dishes

Recipe 11: <u>Simple Crab Legs</u>

| Prep time: 5 minutes | Cook time: 3 minutes | Servings: 5 |

Nutritional Facts Per Serving
- Calories: 152
- Fat: 23g
- Carb: 0g
- Protein: 16g

Ingredients
- Crab legs – 2 pounds, thawed

Method
1. Add 1-cup water into the IP and insert trivet.
2. Place the crab legs on top of the trivet.
3. Press Manual and cook on High for 3 minutes.
4. Do a quick release.
5. Serve crab legs with your favorite sauce.
6. You can pair the recipe with other crab or lobster recipe described in this book.

Recipe 12: Crab Legs with Butter Sauce

| Prep time: 3 minutes | Cook time: 7 minutes | Servings: 2 |

Nutritional Facts Per Serving
- Calories: 511
- Fat: 22.5g
- Carb: 1g
- Protein: 66.7g

Ingredients
- Crab legs – 2 pounds, rinsed
- Water – 1 cup
- Butter – 4 Tbsp.
- Mince garlic – 1 clove
- Lemon – ½, juiced
- Lemon wedges – 4

Method
1. Add water into the Instant Pot.
2. Place steamer basket and crab legs on top.
3. Close the lid and press Steam.
4. Cook 7 minutes.
5. Do a quick release and remove the crab legs.
6. Mix the butter and lemon juice.
7. Serve crab legs with the sauce and lemon wedges.

Recipe 13: Crab Bisque

| Prep time: 5 minutes | Cook time: 3 minutes | Servings: 4 |

Nutritional Facts Per Serving
- Calories: 415
- Fat: 35.1g
- Carb: 8g
- Protein: 13g

Ingredients
- Butter – 4 Tbsp.
- Bone broth – 3 cups
- Full-fat cream cheese – 8 ounces, softened
- Celery – 2 stalks, chopped
- Crab meat – 1 pound, thawed
- Old Bay Seasoning – 1 tsp.
- Cayenne pepper – ½ tsp. ground
- Ground black pepper – ½ tsp.
- Salt – ½ tsp.
- Bell peppers – ¼ cup, chopped
- Heavy whipping cream – ¼ cup
- Small onion – ¼, sliced
- Sugar-free crushed tomatoes – 1 (14-ounce) can

Method
1. Melt the butter on Sauté in the Instant Pot.
2. Pour in the bone broth and add tomatoes, onion, whipping cream, bell pepper, salt, pepper, cayenne pepper, Old Bay, crab, celery, and cream cheese. Mix.
3. Close the lid and cook on Manual for 3 minutes on Low.
4. Do a quick release and open.
5. Blend with a hand mixer.
6. Serve.

Recipe 14: Shrimp, and Crab, with Sausage

| Prep time: 10 minutes | Cook time: 5 minutes | Servings: 4 |

Nutritional Facts Per Serving
- Calories: 239
- Fat: 8g
- Carb: 5.2g
- Protein: 32.2g

Ingredients
- Smoked sausage – ½ pound
- Shelled deveined large shrimp – ½ pound
- Crab legs – 2 pounds
- Seafood stock – 2 cups
- Cajun seasoning – 1 Tbsp.

Method
1. Place all ingredients into the Instant Pot and close the lid.
2. Press Steam and cook 5 minutes.
3. Do a quick release and serve.

Recipe 15: Lemon Butter Lobster Tail

| Prep time: 5 minutes | Cook time: 4 minutes | Servings: 2 |

Nutritional Facts Per Serving
- Calories: 259
- Fat: 17.3g
- Carb: 1g
- Protein: 32.9g

Ingredients
- Chicken broth – 1 cup
- Water – ½ cup
- Old Bay seasoning – 1 tsp.
- Fresh lobster tails – 2 (12-ounce)
- Juice of ½ lemon
- Butter – 2 Tbsp. melted
- Salt – ¼ tsp.
- Dried parsley – ¼ tsp.
- Pepper – 1/8 tsp.

Method
1. Add water, broth, and seasoning into the Instant Pot.
2. Place lobster tails on the steam rack, shell side down.
3. Close the lid and press Manual.
4. Cook 4 minutes on High.
5. Do a quick release.
6. In a bowl, combine salt, pepper, parsley, butter, and lemon juice.
7. Crack open tail and dip into the butter sauce.

Recipe 16: Steamed Lobster Tails

| Prep time: 5 minutes | Cook time: 5 minutes | Servings: 4 |

Nutritional Facts Per Serving
- Calories: 190
- Fat: 12g
- Carb: 0g
- Protein: 19g

Ingredients
- Water – 1 cup
- Butter – ¼ cup, melted
- White wine – ½ cup
- Lobster tails – 4 (washed and cut in half)

Method
1. Place the lobster tails in the steaming basket.
2. Pour the white wine and water into the instant pot and lower the basket.
3. Close the lid and set to Manual.
4. Cook on Low for 4 minutes.
5. Let the pressure come down naturally.
6. Arrange on a platter and drizzle with melted butter.
7. Serve.

Recipe 17: <u>Lobster Bisque</u>

| Prep time: 5 minutes | Cook time: 4 minutes | Servings: 5 |

Nutritional Facts Per Serving
- Calories: 366
- Fat: 18.1g
- Carb: 8g
- Protein: 30.1g

Ingredients
- Lobster tails – 3 (meat removed, chopped and refrigerate, covered)
- Bone broth – 3 cups
- Sugar-free canned diced tomatoes – 3 cups
- Old Bay seasoning – 2 Tbsp.
- Garlic – 1 clove, crushed
- Thyme – 1 tsp. ground
- Hot sauce – 1 tsp.
- Fresh paprika – ½ tsp.
- Salt – ½ tsp.
- Freshly ground black pepper – ½ tsp.
- Heavy whipping cream – 2 cups

Method
1. Place the lobster shells in the Instant Pot.
2. Then add the salt, pepper, paprika, hot sauce, thyme, garlic, Old Bay, tomatoes, and bone broth.
3. Close the lid and press Manual.
4. Cook 4 minutes on High.
5. Do a quick release.
6. Open, remove and discard the shells.
7. Press Keep Warm and mix in whipping cream.
8. Blend with a hand mixer until the mixture becomes smooth.
9. Stir in lobster tails and cover.
10. Press Manual and cook 3 minutes.
11. Do a quick release and open
12. Serve.

Chapter 2.3   Salmon Dishes

Recipe 18: <u>Lemon Dill Salmon</u>

| Prep time: 3 minutes | Cook time: 5 minutes | Servings: 2 |

Nutritional Facts Per Serving
- Calories: 127
- Fat: 4.9g
- Carb: 1.5g
- Protein: 17.1g

Ingredients
- Salmon filets – 2 (3-oz.)
- Chopped fresh dill – 1 tsp.
- Salt – ½ tsp.
- Pepper – ¼ tsp.
- Water – 1 cup
- Lemon juice – 2 Tbsp.
- Lemon – ½, sliced

Method
1. Season the salmon with salt, pepper, and dill.
2. Add water to the Instant Pot and place steam rack.
3. Place salmon on the steam rack (skin side down).
4. Drizzle with lemon juice and put lemon slices on top.
5. Close the lid and press Steam.
6. Cook 5 minutes on High.
7. Do a quick release and serve with lemon slices and dill.

Recipe 19: Salmon Burger with Avocado

| Prep time: 10 minutes | Cook time: 5 minutes | Servings: 4 |

Nutritional Facts Per Serving
- Calories: 425
- Fat: 27.6g
- Carb: 1.3g
- Protein: 35.6g

Ingredients
- Coconut oil - 2 Tbsp.
- Salmon filets - 1 pound, skin removed and finely minced
- Salt - ½ tsp.
- Garlic powder - ¼ tsp.
- Chili powder - ¼ tsp.
- Finely diced onion - 2 Tbsp.
- Egg - 1
- Mayo - 2 Tbsp.
- Ground pork rinds - 1/3 cup
- Avocado - 1, mashed
- Juice of ½ lime

Method
1. Melt the coconut oil on Sauté in the Instant Pot.
2. Place salmon in a bowl.
3. Add remaining ingredients except for lime and avocado.
4. Mix and form 4 patties.
5. Place burgers into the pot and sear 3 to 4 minutes per side.
6. Press Cancel and set aside.
7. Mix lime juice and avocado in a bowl.
8. Divide mash into four sections and place on top of the salmon patties.
9. Serve.

Recipe 20: **Foil Pack Salmon**

| Prep time: 2 minutes | Cook time: 7 minutes | Servings: 2 |

Nutritional Facts Per Serving
- Calories: 125
- Fat: 4.6g
- Carb: 0.4g
- Protein: 18.5g

Ingredients
- Salmon fillets – 2 (3 oz.)
- Salt – 1 tsp.
- Pepper – ¼ tsp.
- Garlic powder – ¼ tsp.
- Dried dill – ¼ tsp.
- Lemon – ½, sliced
- Water – 1 cup

Method
1. Place salmon on a square of foil, skin side down.
2. Season with seasoning and drizzle with lemon juice.
3. Place a lemon slice on each filet.
4. Pour water in the Instant Pot and place a steam rack.
5. Place foil packets on the steam rack and close the lid.
6. Press Steam and cook 7 minutes.
7. Do a quick release and serve.

Recipe 21: <u>Almond Pesto Salmon</u>

| Prep time: 5 minutes | Cook time: 7 minutes | Servings: 4 |

Nutritional Facts Per Serving
- Calories: 182
- Fat: 20.5g
- Carb: 3g
- Protein: 21.2g

Ingredients
- Sliced almonds – ¼ cup
- Butter – 1 Tbsp.
- Salmon fillets – 4 (3-oz.)
- Pesto – ½ cup
- Salt – ½ tsp.
- Pepper – ¼ tsp.
- Water – 1 cup

Method
1. Press Sauté and add butter into the Instant Pot.
2. Sauté almonds for 3 to 5 minutes. Remove and set aside.
3. Season the salmon with salt, pepper, and brush with pesto.
4. Pour water into the Instant Pot and place steam rack.
5. Add salmon to the rack.
6. Close the lid and press Steam.
7. Cook 7 minutes.
8. Serve with almond slices on top.

Recipe 22: Crispy Blackened Salmon

| Prep time: 5 minutes | Cook time: 5 minutes | Servings: 2 |

Nutritional Facts Per Serving
- Calories: 190
- Fat: 11.4g
- Carb: 1g
- Protein: 18.6g

Ingredients
- Salmon filets – 2 (3-ounce)
- Avocado oil – 1 Tbsp.
- Paprika – 1 tsp.
- Salt – ½ tsp.
- Pepper – ¼ tsp.
- Onion powder – ¼ tsp.
- Dried thyme – ¼ tsp.
- Cayenne pepper – 1/8 tsp.

Method
1. Drizzle the salmon with avocado oil.
2. In a bowl, mix remaining ingredients and rub over filets.
3. Press Sauté and place salmon into the Instant Pot.
4. Sear 2 to 5 minutes until seasoning is blackened and serve.

Recipe 23: Salmon with Broccoli

| Prep time: 5 minutes | Cook time: 4 minutes | Servings: 4 |

Nutritional Facts Per Serving
- Calories: 119
- Fat: 5g
- Carb: 4g
- Protein: 16g

Ingredients
- Salmon fillets – 4
- Water – 1 ½ cups
- Broccoli fillets – 10 ounces
- Garlic powder – 1 tsp.
- Salt and pepper to taste

Method
1. Season the salmon with garlic powder, salt, and pepper.
2. Pour the water into the instant pot.
3. Place the salmon in the steaming basket and add the broccoli around the fish.
4. Close the lid and cook on High for 4 minutes.
5. Quick release and serve.

Recipe 24: Salmon with Vegetables

| Prep time: 5 minutes | Cook time: 5 minutes | Servings: 4 |

Nutritional Facts Per Serving
- Calories: 188
- Fat: 8.9g
- Carb: 7g
- Protein: 17.7g

Ingredients
- Fresh parsley – a ½ bunch, plus more for garnish
- Fresh tarragon – 2 to 3 sprigs
- Wild salmon fillets – 1 ½ pound
- Olive oil – 1 Tbsp.
- Sea salt and black pepper to taste
- Lemon – 1, sliced
- Medium zucchinis – 2, julienned
- Medium bell pepper – 2, seeded and julienned
- Medium carrots – 2, julienned

Method
1. Add tarragon, parsley and ¾ cup water into the Instant Pot.
2. Place the steamer rack in the IP.
3. Drizzle the salmon with olive oil and season with salt and pepper.
4. Place the salmon on the rack (skin-side down).
5. Top with lemon slices.
6. Close the lid and press Steam. Steam for 3 minutes.
7. Do a quick release and remove the rack with the salmon. Keep the salmon warm.
8. Keep the liquid and discard the herbs.
9. Add the carrots, peppers, and zucchinis to the IP and close the lid.
10. Press Sauté and cook for 2 to 3 minutes.
11. When the vegetables are tender, remove and season with salt and pepper.
12. Serve.

Recipe 25: Poached Salmon

| Prep time: 5 minutes | Cook time: 3 minutes | Servings: 4 |

Nutritional Facts Per Serving
- Calories: 472
- Fat: 35.3g
- Carb: 4.6g
- Protein: 35.2g

Ingredients
- Lemons- 2, sliced
- Salmon fillets – 4
- Butter- 8 Tbsp. softened
- Dijon mustard – 2 tsp.
- Garlic – 1 clove, chopped
- Thyme – 1 tsp. ground
- Dried parsley – ½ tsp.
- Salt – ½ tsp.
- Freshly ground black pepper - ½ tsp.

Method

1. Add 1-inch water into the Instant Pot.
2. Place the trivet.
3. Place the salmon in an aluminum foil and top with lemon slices.
4. Fold to make a pocket and place on the trivet.
5. Close and cook on Steam for 3 minutes.
6. Meanwhile, melt the butter in the microwave then add salt, pepper, parsley, thyme, garlic, and mustard. Mix well.
7. Do a quick release when done, open and discard the lemon slices.
8. Serve salmon with sauce.

Recipe 26: Sockeye Salmon

| Prep time: 5 minutes | Cook time: 4 minutes | Servings: 4 |

Nutritional Facts Per Serving
- Calories: 195
- Fat: 10g
- Carb: 1g
- Protein: 24g

Ingredients
- Dijon mustard – 1 tsp.
- Garlic powder – 1 tsp.
- Onion powder – ¼ tsp.
- Garlic – 1 clove, minced
- Salmon fillets – 4 (2 to 3 ounce each)
- Lemon juice – 1 tbsp.
- Salt and pepper to taste
- Water – 1 ½ cups

Method
1. Combine the lemon juice, minced garlic, garlic powder, onion powder, and mustard in a small bowl.

2. Brush the mixture over the salmon.

3. Pour the water into the IP and lower the rack.

4. Arrange the salmon on the rack and close the lid.

5. Cook on High for 4 minutes.

6. Do a quick pressure release and serve.

Recipe 27: Italian Salmon

| Prep time: 5 minutes | Cook time: 3 minutes | Servings: 4 |

Nutritional Facts Per Serving
- Calories: 470
- Fat: 31g
- Carb: 4.6g
- Protein: 43g

Ingredients
- Salmon fillets – 4 (2 to 3 ounces each)
- Water – 1 cup
- Rosemary sprig – 1
- Olive oil – 2 tbsp.
- Italian seasoning – 1 tsp.
- Pepper – ¼ tsp.
- Salt – ¼ tsp.
- Garlic powder – ¼ tsp.
- Halved cherry tomatoes – 1 cup
- Asparagus spears – 15 ounces

Method
1. Pour the water into the Instant Pot.
2. Season the salmon with Italian seasoning, garlic powder, pepper, and salt.
3. Arrange on the rack.
4. Add the rosemary sprig on top.
5. Place the asparagus spears over.
6. Top with cherry tomatoes.
7. Close the lid and cook on High for 3 minutes.
8. Do a quick release and transfer to a plate.
9. Drizzle with olive oil
10. Serve.

Chapter 2.4   Tuna & Cod Dishes

Recipe 28: Garlic Tuna Patties

| Prep time: 10 minutes | Cook time: 10 minutes | Servings: 6 |

Nutritional Facts Per Serving
- Calories: 248
- Fat: 4g
- Carb: 2g
- Protein: 7g

Ingredients
- Dill – 1 tsp. chopped
- Garlic powder – 1 tsp.
- Olive oil – 1 Tbsp.
- Water – ½ cup
- Canned tuna – 15 ounces, drain and flaked
- Parsley – 1 tsp. chopped
- Red onion – ½ cup, chopped
- Salt and pepper to taste
- Eggs – 3

Method
1. In a bowl, mix the eggs, garlic powder, onion, parsley, dill, salt, pepper, and tuna.
2. Combine well and shape into patties.
3. Press Sauté on your Instant Pot and add oil. Cook the patties for 2 minutes. Transfer to a plate.
4. Clean the Instant Pot and add water. Add the steamer basket and add tuna patties inside.
5. Close the pot and press Manual. Cook for 6 minutes.
6. Do a quick release.
7. Serve.

Recipe 29: Almond Tuna

| Prep time: 5 minutes | Cook time: 3 minutes | Servings: 4 |

Nutritional Facts Per Serving
- Calories: 150
- Fat: 5g
- Carb: 4g
- Protein: 10g

Ingredients
- Tuna – 2 cups, drained
- Shaved almonds – 1 cup
- Butter – 2 tbsp.
- Garlic powder – 1 tsp.
- Grated Cheddar Cheese – 1 cup

Method
1. Melt the butter in the instant pot on Sauté.
2. Add cheddar, tuna, and almonds.
3. Cook on Sauté for 3 minutes.
4. Serve over cauliflower rice.

Recipe 30: <u>Olive Cod Mystery</u>

| Prep time: 8 minutes | Cook time: 10 minutes | Servings: 4 |

Nutritional Facts Per Serving
- Calories: 185
- Fat: 3g
- Carb: 6g
- Protein: 7g

Ingredients
- Water – 1 cup
- Capers – 2 Tbsp. chopped
- Black olives – 1 cup, pitted and chopped
- Cherry tomatoes – 17 ounces, halved
- Cod fillets – 4, boneless and skinless
- Garlic – 1 clove, minced
- Olive oil – 1 Tbsp.
- Salt and pepper to taste
- Parsley – 1 Tbsp. finely chopped

Method
1. In a dish, mix the garlic, capers, olives, fish, oil, parsley, salt, pepper, and tomatoes. Toss to combine well.

2. Pour the water in the Instant Pot and place a trivet. Arrange the dish over the trivet.

3. Close the pot and press Manual. Cook for 8 minutes.

4. Do a quick release.

5. Serve.

Recipe 31: Tomato Cod

| Prep time: 5 minutes | Cook time: 15 minutes | Servings: 4 |

Nutritional Facts Per Serving
- Calories: 157
- Fat: 7.3g
- Carb: 2.2g
- Protein: 21g

Ingredients
- Butter – 2 Tbsp.
- Diced onion – ¼ cup
- Minced garlic – 1 clove
- Cherry tomatoes – 1 cup, chopped
- Salt – ¼ tsp.
- Pepper – 1/8 tsp.
- Dried thyme – ¼ tsp.
- Chicken broth – ¼ cup
- Capers – 1 Tbsp.
- Cod filets – 4 (4-oz.)
- Water – 1 cup
- Chopped parsley – ¼ cup

Method
1. Melt the butter on Sauté in the instant pot.
2. Add onion and stir-fry until soften.
3. Add garlic and cook 30 seconds more.
4. Add broth, thyme, pepper, salt, and chopped tomatoes.
5. Cook 5 to 7 minutes or until tomatoes soften. Press Cancel.
6. Pour sauce into a bowl.
7. Add fish fillets and capers. Cover with foil.
8. Pour water into the Instant Pot.
9. Place steam rack on the bottom.
10. Place bowl on top.
11. Close the lid and press Manual.
12. Cook 3 minutes.
13. Do a quick release.
14. Sprinkle with fresh parsley and serve.

Recipe 32: Coconut Milk Cod

| Prep time: 5 minutes | Cook time: 13 minutes | Servings: 4 |

Nutritional Facts Per Serving
- Calories: 260
- Fat: 14g
- Carb: 6.1g
- Protein: 24g

Ingredients
- Cod fillets – 1 pound
- Almond flour – 3 tbsp.
- Lime zest – 1 tbsp.
- Minced garlic – 1 tsp.
- Butter – 1 tbsp.
- Soy sauce – 2 tbsp.
- Fish sauce – ¼ cup
- Coconut milk – ½ cup

Method
1. Chop the cod and insert in the instant pot.
2. Add the remaining ingredients and stir to combine.
3. Set the instant pot to sauté and close the lid.
4. Cover and lock the lid and cook for 10 minutes on Sauté.
5. Open the lid and cook for 3 minutes more and serve.

Chapter 2.5   Other Fishes Dishes

Recipe 33: <u>Creamy Haddock</u>

| Prep time: 5 minutes | Cook time: 10 minutes | Servings: 4 |

Nutritional Facts Per Serving
- Calories: 195
- Fat: 18g
- Carb: 5.5g
- Protein: 18g

Ingredients
- Haddock fillets – 12 ounces
- Butter – 1 tbsp.
- Heavy cream – ½ cup
- Cheddar cheese – 5 ounces, grated
- Diced onions – 3 tbsp.
- Garlic salt – ¼ tsp.
- Pepper – ¼ tsp.

Method
1. On Sauté setting, melt the butter in the instant pot.
2. Sauté the onions for 2 minutes.
3. Season the fish with salt and pepper.
4. Place in the instant pot and cook for 2 minutes per side.
5. Pour the cream over and top with the cheese.
6. Cook on Manual for 5 minutes.
7. Do natural pressure release.
8. Serve.

Recipe 34: Haddock and Cheddar

| Prep time: 5 minutes | Cook time: 10 minutes | Servings: 4 |

Nutritional Facts Per Serving
- Calories: 195
- Fat: 18g
- Carb: 5.5g
- Protein: 18g

Ingredients
- Haddock fillets – 12 ounces
- Butter – 1 tbsp.
- Heavy cream – ½ cup
- Cheddar cheese – 5 ounces, grated
- Diced onions – 3 tbsp.
- Garlic salt – ¼ tsp.
- Pepper – ¼ tsp.

Method
1. Melt the butter in the IP on Sauté.
2. Sauté the onions for 2 minutes.
3. Season the fish with salt and pepper.
4. Place in the IP and cook for 2 minutes per side.
5. Pour the cream over and top with the cheese.
6. Cook on Manual for 5 minutes.
7. Do a natural pressure release and serve.

Recipe 35: Caramelized Tilapia

| Prep time: 30 minutes | Cook time: 10 minutes | Servings: 4 |

Nutritional Facts Per Serving
- Calories: 150
- Fat: 4g
- Carb: 3g
- Protein: 21g

Ingredients
- Tilapia fillets – 1 pound
- Red chili – 1, minced
- Minced garlic – 3 tsp.
- Granulated sweetener – ¼ tsp.
- Spring onion – 1, minced
- Coconut water – ¾ cup
- Water – 1/3 cup
- Fish sauce – 3 tbsp.
- Salt and pepper to taste

Method
1. Combine the garlic, fish sauce, salt, and pepper in a bowl.
2. Place the tilapia inside and mix to coat.
3. Cover and let sit in the fridge for 30 minutes.
4. Meanwhile, combine the water and sweetener in the instant pot.
5. Cook on Sauté until caramelized.
6. Add fish and pour the coconut water over.
7. Close and lock the lid. Cook on High for 10 minutes.
8. Do a quick pressure release.
9. Top the fish with spring onion and chili.
10. Serve.

Recipe 36: Mackerel with Tomatoes

| Prep time: 5 minutes | Cook time: 5 minutes | Servings: 4 |

Nutritional Facts Per Serving
- Calories: 400
- Fat: 17g
- Carb: 3.5g
- Protein: 40g

Ingredients
- Cherry tomatoes – 2 cups
- Mackerel fillets – 4
- Water – 1 ½ cups
- Butter – 2 tbsp. melted
- Garlic salt – ¼ tsp.
- Onion powder – ¼ tsp.
- Pepper – ¼ tsp.

Method
1. Place the tomatoes in a baking dish.
2. Arrange the mackerel over.
3. Drizzle with butter and sprinkle with spices.
4. Pour the water into the Instant Pot and lower the trivet.
5. Place the baking dish inside and close the lid.
6. Cook on High for 5 minutes.
7. Do a quick pressure release and serve.

Recipe 37: Fish Taco Bowls

| Prep time: 15 minutes | Cook time: 5 minutes | Servings: 4 |

Nutritional Facts Per Serving
- Calories: 328
- Fat: 23.8g
- Carb: 4.2g
- Protein: 19.4g

Ingredients
- Shredded cabbage – 4 cups
- Mayo – ¼ cup
- Sour cream – 2 Tbsp.
- Lime – 1, halved
- Chopped pickled jalapenos – 2 Tbsp.
- Tilapia filets – 3 (4-oz.)
- Chili powder – 2 tsp.
- Cumin – 1 tsp.
- Garlic powder – 1 tsp.
- Salt – 1 tsp.
- Coconut oil – 2 Tbsp.
- Avocado – 1, diced
- Chopped cilantro – 4 Tbsp.

Method
1. Mix jalapenos, juice of half lime, sour cream, mayo, and cabbage in a bowl.
2. Cover and keep in the refrigerator for 30 minutes.
3. Press Sauté and add coconut oil to the Instant Pot.
4. Season the filets with seasonings.
5. Add filets and sear 2 to 4 minutes on each side.
6. Press Cancel.
7. Chop fish into bite-sized pieces.
8. Divided slaw into four bowls and place fish on top.
9. Add chopped avocado, drizzle with lime juice.
10. Sprinkle with cilantro and serve.

Recipe 38: Herbed Catfish

| Prep time: 5 minutes | Cook time: 6 minutes | Servings: 4 |

Nutritional Facts Per Serving
- Calories: 160
- Fat: 10g
- Carb: 2.4g
- Protein: 18g

Ingredients
- Catfish fillets – 14 ounces
- Olive oil – 1 tbsp.
- Chopped parsley – 1 tsp.
- Fresh thyme – ¼ cup
- Dill – 1 tsp.
- Water – ¼ cup
- Fish stock – ½ cup
- Soy sauce – 2 tbsp.
- Minced garlic – 2 tsp.
- Salt – 1 tsp.

Method
1. Chop the fish and place in the instant pot.
2. Add the remaining ingredients and stir to combine.
3. Close the lid and press the manual.
4. Cook on High for 5 minutes.
5. Press cancel and do a quick pressure release.
6. Set it to Sauté and cook for 1 more minute with the lid off.
7. Serve.

Recipe 39: White Fish Stew

| Prep time: 5 minutes | Cook time: 8 minutes | Servings: 6 |

Nutritional Facts Per Serving
- Calories: 165
- Fat: 13g
- Carb: 5g
- Protein: 24g

Ingredients
- Onion – 1, diced
- Carrot – 1, sliced
- Celery stalks – 2, diced
- Heavy cream – 1 cup
- Whitefish fillets – 1 pound
- Fish broth – 3 cups
- Chopped broccoli – 1 cup
- Chopped cauliflower – 1 cup
- Chopped kale – 1 cup
- Butter – 2 tbsp.
- Salt and pepper to taste

Method
1. Melt the butter in the instant pot on Sauté.
2. Sauté the onions for 3 minutes.
3. Except for the cream, stir all of the ingredients.
4. Close the lid and press Manual.
5. Cook on High for 5 minutes.
6. Do a natural pressure release.
7. Stir in the heavy cream.
8. Discard the bay leaf and serve.

Recipe 40: Mahi Mahi

| Prep time: 5 minutes | Cook time: 4 minutes | Servings: 4 |

Nutritional Facts Per Serving
- Calories: 310
- Fat: 11.4g
- Carb: 1.3g
- Protein: 47.4g

Ingredients
- Butter – 3 Tbsp. softened
- Grated ginger – 1 piece
- Lime – ½, juiced
- Lemon – ½, juiced
- Dried basil – ½ tsp.
- Black pepper – ½ tsp.
- Salt – ½ tsp.
- Minced garlic – ½ tsp.
- Mahi Mahi fillets – 4

Method
1. Add ½ cup water into the Instant Pot.
2. Insert the trivet.
3. Combine garlic, salt, black pepper, basil, lemon juice, lime juice, ginger, and butter in a bowl. Mix well.
4. Coat the fish with this mixture.
5. Grease a dish and place fillets on it.
6. Place the dish on the trivet and cover loosely with aluminum foil.
7. Close the lid.
8. Press Manual and cook 4 minutes on Low.
9. Once cooked do a natural pressure release.
10. Open and serve.

Recipe 41: Dijon Halibut

| Prep time: 5 minutes | Cook time: 3 minutes | Servings: 4 |

Nutritional Facts Per Serving
- Calories: 190
- Fat: 2g
- Carb: 0.1g
- Protein: 40g

Ingredients
- Dijon mustard – 1 ½ Tbsp.
- Halibut fillets – 4
- Water – 1 ½ cups

Method
1. Pour the water into the IP.
2. Brush the halibut with Dijon and place in the steaming basket.
3. Lower the basket and close the lid.
4. Set the IP to Manual.
5. Cook on High for 3 minutes.
6. Do a quick pressure release.
7. Serve.

Recipe 42: Trout Casserole

| Prep time: 5 minutes | Cook time: 20 minutes | Servings: 4 |

Nutritional Facts Per Serving
- Calories: 361
- Fat: 23.8g
- Carb: 3.7g
- Protein: 31.6g

Ingredients
- Trout fillets – 1 lb. without skin
- Cherry tomatoes – 1 cup, halved
- Zucchini – ½, sliced
- Cauliflower – 1 cup, chopped into florets
- Small onion – 1, sliced
- Olive oil – 4 tbsp.

Spices
- Sea salt – 2 tsp.
- Dried rosemary -1 tsp.
- Dried thyme – 1 tsp.
- Garlic powder – ½ tsp.

Method
1. Line a small square pan with some parchment paper and sprinkle with two tablespoons of olive oil.

2. Arrange onions at the bottom of the pan and make a layer with zucchini. Top with onions and cherry tomatoes. Drizzle with oil and sprinkle with salt.

3. Top with trout fillets and season with garlic powder, thyme, rosemary, and more salt.

4. Tightly wrap with aluminum foil and set aside.

5. Pour in 2 cups of water in the IP. Set the trivet at the bottom of the inner pot and place the pan on top.

6. Seal the lid and press Manual. Set the timer for 20 minutes on high pressure.

7. When cooked, do a quick pressure release and open the lid.

8. Carefully open the pan and chill for a while.

9. Remove the aluminum foil and optionally, bake for 15 minutes at 450F.

10. Serve.

Chapter 2.6 Other Seafood Dishes

Recipe 43: Wonder Wine Clams

| Prep time: 10 minutes | Cook time: 8 minutes | Servings: 4 |

Nutritional Facts Per Serving
- Calories: 226
- Fat: 14g
- Carb: 5.5g
- Protein: 14.5g

Ingredients
- Clams – 2 ½ pounds, scrubbed
- Lemon juice – 2 Tbsp.
- Vegetable broth – 2 cups
- White wine – ¼ cup
- Olive oil – ¼ cup
- Garlic – 2 cloves, minced
- Chopped basil – ¼ cup

Method
1. Press Sauté and add oil. Add the garlic and stir-fry for 2 minutes.
2. Add wine, lemon juice, broth, and basil and bring to a boil for 1 minute.
3. Arrange the trivet and place the clams over the trivet.
4. Close the pot and press Manual. Cook for 4 minutes.
5. Do a quick release and open.
6. Remove the clams that haven't opened.
7. Place the clams on a serving plate. Pour the liquid over and serve.

Recipe 44: Steamed Clams

| Prep time: 5 minutes | Cook time: 5 minutes | Servings: 4 |

Nutritional Facts Per Serving
- Calories: 151
- Fat: 11g
- Carb: 2.1g
- Protein: 8.7g

Ingredients
- Clams – 2 pounds
- Seafood stock – 1 cup
- Butter – 4 Tbsp.

Method
1. Place seafood stock and clams into the Instant Pot.
2. Close the lid.
3. Press Steam and cook 5 minutes.
4. Do a quick release.
5. Serve with butter.

Recipe 45: Clambake

| Prep time: 5 minutes | Cook time: 6 minutes | Servings: 4 |

Nutritional Facts Per Serving
- Calories: 137
- Fat: 2g
- Carb: 3g
- Protein: 26.1g

Ingredients
- Avocado oil – 2 Tbsp.
- Bone broth – 1 cup
- Clams – 20, scrubbed
- Lobster tails – 2, thawed if frozen
- Salt – ½ tsp.
- Freshly ground black pepper to taste

Method
1. Press Sauté and heat the oil.
2. Add the bone broth in the Instant Pot.
3. Add the lobster tails, clams, salt, and pepper to the Instant Pot. Working in batches if necessary.
4. Close the lid and hit Cancel.
5. Press Manual and cook 6 minutes on High.
6. Do a natural release and remove lobster tails and clams and serve.

Recipe 46: Buttered Scallops

| Prep time: 5 minutes | Cook time: 5 minutes | Servings: 4 |

Nutritional Facts Per Serving
- Calories: 190
- Fat: 12.4g
- Carb: 3.7g
- Protein: 13.7g

Ingredients
- Avocado oil – 2 Tbsp.
- Large sea scallops – 1 pound, prepared
- Salt – 1/8 tsp.
- Pepper – 1/8 tsp.
- Melted butter – 2 Tbsp.

Method
1. Press Sauté and heat the avocado oil in the Instant Pot.
2. Season scallops with salt and pepper.
3. Sear scallops 2 to 3 minutes on each side.
4. Pour butter over scallops and serve hot.

Recipe 47: Oysters

| Prep time: 5 minutes | Cook time: 3 minutes | Servings: 6 |

Nutritional Facts Per Serving
- Calories: 145
- Fat: 12g
- Carb: 1g
- Protein: 13g

Ingredients
- Water – 1 cup
- Oysters – 36 (cleaned)
- Melted butter – 6 tbsp.

Method
1. Place the oysters in the instant pot.
2. Pour the water and close the lid.
3. Cook on High for 3 minutes.
4. Do a natural pressure release.
5. Transfer to a serving plate.
6. Drizzle with the melted butter and serve.

Recipe 48: Seafood Gumbo

| Prep time: 5 minutes | Cook time: 15 minutes | Servings: 6 |

Nutritional Facts Per Serving
- Calories: 365
- Fat: 14g
- Carb: 10g
- Protein: 41g

Ingredients
- Sea bass fillets – 2 pounds, cut into bite-sized pieces
- Shrimp – 2 pounds, peeled, and deveined
- Sweet bell peppers – 2, finely chopped
- Celery ribs – 4, chopped
- Bay leaves – 3
- Fish stock – 1 ½ cup
- Diced tomatoes -1 (28-ounce) can
- Tomato paste – ¼ cup
- Avocado oil – 3 Tbsp.
- Medium yellow onions – 2, chopped
- Cilantro – ¼ cup, freshly chopped
- Cajun seasoning – 3 Tbsp.
- Sea salt – 1 tsp.
- Freshly ground black pepper – 1 tsp.

Method
1. Season the sea bass fillets with half of the Cajun seasoning, salt, and black pepper.
2. Press the Sauté and add the oil.
3. Add the fish pieces to the hot oil and cook until lightly browned on each side, about 3 minutes. Remove.
4. Add bell peppers, celery, onions, and remaining Cajun seasoning to the Instant Pot. Sauté until softened, about 3 minutes. Stirring occasionally. Turn off Sauté.
5. Return the cooked fish to the Instant Pot along with the fish stock, bay leaves, tomato paste, and tomatoes. Mix well.
6. Cover the pot and press Manual. Cook 5 minutes on High.
7. Do a quick release and open the lid.
8. Stir the shrimp and cook until pink and opaque.
9. Season with salt, and black pepper. Top with fresh cilantro.
10. Serve.

Recipe 49: Seafood Paella

| Prep time: 5 minutes | Cook time: 8 minutes | Servings: 4 |

Nutritional Facts Per Serving
- Calories: 156
- Fat: 4.5g
- Carb: 5g
- Protein: 15g

Ingredients
- Chopped fish – 1 cup
- Shellfish – 2 cups (calms, mussels, shrimp)
- Cauliflower rice – 2 cups
- Red bell pepper – 1, diced
- Ghee – 1 tbsp.
- Green bell pepper – 1, diced
- Onion – 1, sliced
- Fish stock – 4 cups
- A pinch of saffron
- Salt and pepper to taste

Method
1. Melt the ghee in the IP.
2. Add peppers and onion and cook for 3 minutes.
3. Stir in the stock, rice, fish, and saffron.
4. Close the lid and cook for 2 minutes on High.
5. Release pressure naturally.
6. Add the shellfish (do not stir) and close the lid.
7. Cook for 3 minutes more.
8. Let the pressure drop naturally.
9. Serve.

Recipe 50: Seafood Stew

| Prep time: 5 minutes | Cook time: 13 minutes | Servings: 5 |

Nutritional Facts Per Serving
- Calories: 433
- Fat: 18.5g
- Carb: 4.6g
- Protein: 58.5g

Ingredients
- Sea bass fillets – 2 lbs. cut into chunks
- Shrimps – 7 oz. peeled and deveined
- Large onion – 1, finely chopped
- Olive oil – 4 tbsp. extra-virgin
- Celery – 3 stalks, finely chopped
- Small tomatoes – 2, chopped
- Liquid aminos – 3 tbsp.
- Fish stock – 5 cups

Spices
- Sea salt – 2 tsp.
- Black pepper – 1 tsp. ground
- Bay leaves – 2
- Creole seasoning – 1 tbsp.

Method

1. Clean and rinse fish fillets. Pat dry with paper towels and set aside.

2. Combine the seasoning and salt and pepper in a bowl. Rub the fish with this mixture and coat well.

3. Press Sauté on your IP. Grease the inner pot with olive oil and heat up.

4. Add the prepared fish and cook for 4 to 5 minutes, stirring occasionally.

5. Once the fish is browned, remove from the pot and set aside.

6. Grease the inner pot with more oil and add celery stalk and onions. Season with salt and stir well. Cook for 2 to 3 minutes.

7. Press Cancel and add the tomatoes, shrimps, and fish. Drizzle with liquid amions and pour in the stock.

8. Seal the lid and set the steam release handle to the Sealing position. Press the Manual and set the timer for 5 minutes on High Pressure.

9. Once cooked, release pressure naturally and open the lid.

10. Stir in some fresh parsley and serve.

CHAPTER 3: CONCLUSION

Cooking fish and other seafood at home is much easier than you think! This cookbook includes exciting recipes for the worlds' healthiest proteins. Much more than a cookbook, this is an ultimate guide for every home cook who loves cooking and eating fish and seafood. This is the only guide you will ever need to professionally cook a variety of fish and seafood.

-- Johanna Davis

Made in the USA
San Bernardino, CA
04 March 2020